Also by BRETT RUTHERFORD

POETRY
Songs of the I and Thou (1968)
City Limits (1970)
The Pumpkined Heart: Pennsylvania Poems (1973, 2012)
Thunderpuss: In Memoriam (1987)
Prometheus on Fifth Avenue (1987)
At Lovecraft's Grave (1988)
In Chill November (1990)
Poems from Providence (1991, 2011)
Twilight of the Dictators (with Pieter Vanderbeck) (1992, 2009)
Knecht Ruprecht, or the Bad Boy's Christmas (1992)
The Gods As They Are, On Their Planets (2005, 2012)
Things Seen in Graveyards (2007)
Doctor Jones and Other Terrors (2008)
Anniversarius: The Book of Autumn (1984, 1986, 1996, 2011)
An Expectation of Presences (2012)

PLAYS
Night Gaunts: An Entertainment Based on the Life and Work of H.P. Lovecraft (1993, 2005)

NOVELS
Piper (with John Robertson) (1985)
The Lost Children (1988)

AS EDITOR/PUBLISHER
May Eve: A Festival of Supernatural Poems (1975)
Last Flowers: The Romance Poems of Edgar Allan Poe and Sarah Helen Whitman (1987, 2003, 2008, 2011)
M.G. Lewis's *Tales of Wonder*. Annotated edition. (2010, 2012)
A.T. Fitzroy. *Despised and Rejected*. Annotated edition. (2010)
Death and the Downs: The Poetry of Charles Hamilton Sorley. Annotated edition. (2010)

Trilobite Love Song

NEW POEMS & REVISIONS 2013-2014

BRETT RUTHERFORD

THE POET'S PRESS
PITTSBURGH, PA

Copyright © 2014 by Brett Rutherford
Second printing April 2017
All Rights Reserved
ISBN 0-922558-76-0
The author places this work in the Public Domain
on January 1, 2032.

"Hoxie House" previously appeared in
Sensations Magazine

Rev 1.2

This is the 209th publication of
THE POET'S PRESS
2209 Murray Avenue #3/ Pittsburgh, PA 15217
www.poetspress.org

TABLE OF CONTENTS

The Special Ward at Butler Hospital 9
Trilobite Love Song 12
At Innsmouth Harbor 14
Alexander Pushkin: The Demons 16
Hoxie House 19
On the Island of Pohnpei 21
Providence Nocturne: Two Portraits 25
A Year and a Day 29
What She Was Like 31
Anna Akhmatova: That Moment 35
Lines Overheard 37
Intro to Literary Theory 38
Old Poet Glimpsed on the Subway 40
Young Girl's Prayer to Eos, at Corinth 42

FOUR POEMS OF LI YÜ
Down South 46
Fisherman 47
Exile, Under the New Moon 49
Assignation 51

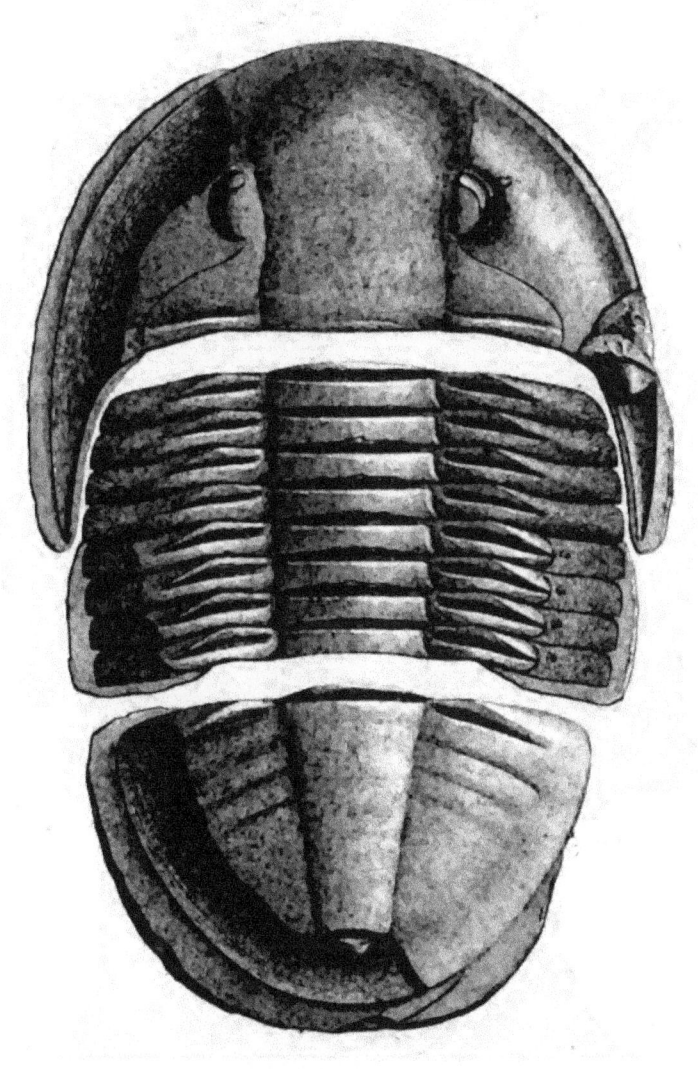

TRILOBITE LOVE SONG

THE SPECIAL WARD
AT BUTLER HOSPITAL

Ah, here we are. For the state of these hallways
I must apologize. The janitors won't clean here:
It's in their contract since the 1930s. We make do.
There's nothing really down here, you see. I'm sure
You'll want to see our new outpatient clinic. No?
Ward B? A *special* ward? Can't say I know of it.
These doors are locked. They're *always* locked.
There's nothing to see there, really. Inspector,
we've done the annual visit the same each year.
You've never asked about this basement. Oh?
An inquiry? Grand jury, you say? I'm sorry, no:
I'm not allowed to open this. Subpoena? I see;
Yes, yes, it all seems clearly worded: "Ward B,
Locked rooms in Butler's basement. Inspect."
I still don't think I'm authorized to open — ah,
I see your two friends' badges there, and, oh,
I'd rather you not display those handguns
considering our population here. Ward B.
The key is here somewhere. You're making me
exceedingly nervous with that .38. Wrong key.
Damn! Here it is! It's open! It's open!
You'll need a moment to adjust to the dimness.

The men are on this side,
    behind the plexiglass.
There's a certain family likeness for some:
those lantern jaws, that gait aloof and awkward,
all dressed in their grandfathers' suits.
Every one of them thinks he's H. P. Lovecraft.
Untreatable, incurable (and certainly unemployable);
nothing short of lobotomy will pull them out of it.
Last count, three hundred. They come from everywhere.

Most states outsource their Lovecraft maniacs:
Their loss, our gain. At least it's easy to feed them.
Crackers and chili, a slice of pie.
They're calm except for those nights
On which we bring them ice cream.
They eat it off each other's bodies, something
you'd pay me not to have to watch.

The Lovecraft women are on the other side.
No, only a dozen or so right now. They suicide
as fast as we get them in. The "Howards"
are not remotely interested in meeting them.
Some lie there at night, exposing themselves
toward the Hyades; some play with rats
and give them endearing little names.
Most of them just read, and lick the wallpaper,
and fill up the room with plush toy octopi
(we sell them in the gift store up above).
A number of them turn out, on closer inspection,
to actually be men. We call them Cthulhu's nuns.
Every woman who ever reads Lovecraft
winds up this way. They really should ban him.

Here in the back, we have the "machinery."
There's the lobotomy kit, and over there
the latest in electroshock, but as I said,
they're pretty much incurable. Just take a look:
they're not particularly unhappy. They read;
endless long letters they write to imaginary friends
(of course we never mail them); and they dispute
among themselves for hours fine points
of eldritch lore and Arkham geography.

Report what you like. I think we're kind to them.
Back in the 60s a former director said, "Empty the place,"
and so we had them all drafted to the infantry:
imagine a platoon of Lovecrafts in Vietnam!
This is not a bad life. It's not as though
they could go out and get jobs, you know.

So that's the tour. Gentlemen, your guns.
Thank you for bringing the Inspector down
without his being any the wiser. Just tie him down
to that bed by the electroshock. There, there,
Inspector, it will be fine before long. Your boss
is repressing all evidence of that sacrifice you made
during your South Pacific vacation last year —
all that mess, *tsk! tsk!* and no Cthulhu
to show for your trouble. You'll be all right.
You're going to have three hundred best friends,
and they'll be just like you. You could live
to a hundred down here. All those books to read
and we even have our own closed-circuit TV:
all Lovecraft, all the time. And now, stop talking.
I'll just tape over your mouth so you can listen.
Just for you. The rats. The rats in the wall.

TRILOBITE LOVE SONG

My thousand eyes are upon you.
Even when I molt, when others would dream
in an agony of pain denial, I stay alert.
I watch for your every passing.
Everything I sense about you
    from infrared to ultraviolet
        is in perfect focus at every distance.
Not even a feeding cave or a narrow crevice
can hide you from me: I know
the subtle song of your feet and feelers.
The mottled markings on your thorax
make me go rugose: I cannot help it.
The intricate spines of your cranidium,
stretching like the finest sea-flower,
drive me to impolite excesses.
    (Oh I have mapped them and would
    ten times trace them with my ten
    appendages if only you would permit it!)

Greater order, you
    have never noticed me,
    a bottom-feeder for all you know.
Yet I have followed you for years now.
I listened silently as you and all those others
formed into a linked circle, a thousand-feeler,
ten-thousand spine symphony of singing.
I think the earth stopped in its orbit
when you played the *click-click-click* symphony
of the revered master *click-rrr — click-rrr — click — ahk*.
All I could so was weep inside my calcite lenses
and let my spines go limp.

How could you know my dream of you
    inspired me to swim higher
    beyond the blue-green fringe water
    into the blazing Greater Light,
where I lay gasping with salt-dry gills
    click-clicking your name

as the Greater Light plummeted
    and the blue-white Lesser Light
    stole in to replace it —
just so do I, the lesser, pursue you.

I am not worth
    one twitch of your pygidium tail
but I am convinced of a destiny
since ever I first looked upon you.
I guard your molting against all predators,
though you have never known it.
When I was younger, I traced
lewd messages on the sand floor,
wiping them out as fast as I wrote them —
oh, things that would embarrass you,
one typical juvenile verse went something like:

> *I want to hold my click-click*
> *against your click-click-ack-click*
> *until we grrrr-te-te*

So as you see, I am not much of a poet,
even less a courtier. My only hope
is that you have held yourself aloof,
that perhaps in your greater essence
is a greater shyness. Or, hope of hopes,
that you have seen me all along,
and only need my boldness. Oh, dare I?

Without your prior enrollment and slow
unrolling, without that stretch of feelers
and the ensuing embarement of thorax,
dare I approach and say the words
of surrender and engagement:

Thou, greater than me, and whom I love:
I lay my eggs at your feet.

AT INNSMOUTH HARBOR

The catalog of jetsam —
things washed ashore at Innsmouth:
a gnawed-through baby rattle; five
matched silver spoons of serpentine design;
a multitude of basalt pebbles, each
a perfect copy of its brethren, angled
obtuse with the hint of an eye,
black and unseeing (on the obverse,
an alien cuneiform, unreadable),
coins all of an unknown empire;
the rusted machinery of lost umbrellas
(from where since no one ever in Innsmouth
has ever owned or needed one);
clots of dank seaweed and curds of ooze
astir with phosphorescent pulsings;
a human skeleton, a chain, a cinder block;
blue bottle, labeled *Tincture of Laudanum*,
wrapped in soft velvet with an ivory carving,
priapic secret of a ship captain's widow;
an octopus impaled with the periscope
of a German U-2 submarine; a map
of the New England coastline inscribed
entirely in Runic letters; a trident,
vertical, twelve feet from top to bottom,
awaiting whoever dares to claim it;
and finally, as always, coats, hats and trousers,
all manner of ladies' gowns and negligée
cast off on the rocks at Devil's Reef,
all for the taking if anyone cares.

There is no catalog of flotsam, no list
of the things that will not come to shore:
the ten-lobed all-seeing eyes of the ghosts
of Trilobites, mandarins of the ocean deep;
the wary, watchful ammoniac waiting
of *Architeuthis*, the giant squid; the pound
and beat of the tide-drum, counting all down
to the world's end, the sun's death, the pull
of all into the dark heart of the iron stone
where everything that was and will be comes to rest.

ALEXANDER PUSHKIN: THE DEMONS

The clouds whirl, the clouds scurry.
The moon, unseen, lights up
from above the flying snow.
Gloom-ridden sky, gloom-ridden night:
on my life, I can't find the way.
I drive, I drive on the endless steppe.
The little bell's *ding-ding-ding*
flies back to me, fearsome,
fearsome in spite of one's self,
lost bells amid an unknown plain!

— "Driver, don't stop! Keep going on!" —
— "It's impossible, sir. It's a heavy go
for the horses against all this snow.
And my eyes are swelling shut, sir.
Who can make out where snow ends
and where the land begins?
All the roads are covered, I swear.
Kill me if you like. I've stopped,
for not a track is to be seen.
We are lost! What would you have me do?" —

— "What have you been following, driver,
if you can see no road?" —
— "Some Demon of the steppe, my lord,
is leading the horse and me. I thought
I recognized a turn or two, but no,
now we've been turned aside. We're lost!

"Look, there ahead beyond that drift
he huffs, and spits at me. My God,
he's almost led the stumbling team
into a steep ravine! Back, back!

"Did you not see him, sir? He stood
as thin as a weird mile-post before us.
(Here, take this cloth and clean
your fogged-up spectacles!)
Look there — that little spark was him,
and now he's gone into the empty dark."

The clouds whirl, the clouds scurry.
The moon, unseen, lights up
from above the flying snow.
Gloom-ridden sky, gloom-ridden night:
on my life, I can't find the way.
We have no strength to go onward:
there, look, our tracks again:
we have gone in a full circle!
The little bell is suddenly silent,
in a fog so thick it cannot tremble.
The horses stop. What is that in the field?

"Who knows, sir. It's just a tree stump.
No, *Bozhe moi*, I see a wolf!"
The snowstorm becomes furious,
the snowstorm howls and wails.
The snorting horses make sounds
of terror and try to break the reins.

"There — farther on — the Demon.
I saw him jump, sir. See there:
just those two eyes float deep,
red lamps inside the gray-white
nothingness of sky and snow."

Then comes a sudden silence,
a narrow path made visible
lures on the horses; the bell
makes tentative tinkles. I see
a line of phantoms assembled
on either side of us,
in the midst of the whitening plains.

Onward we go, the driver's
whispered litany of *Bozhe moi,*
Bozhe moi and the silver ding
of the blessed sledge-bell
our only prow and pilot.
Endless and formless,
the Demons watch us
in the dim play of the moonlight;
they are are legion as leaves
on the ground in November.

How many are there? Where do they go
en masse in this blizzard night?
And, oh, they are singing. Hush, driver!
Listen to that plaintive melody!
Are they off to some hobgoblins' burial?
Is Baba Yaga at last to be married?

The clouds whirl, the clouds scurry.
The moon, unseen, lights up
from above the flying snow.
Gloom-ridden sky, gloom-ridden night:
on my life, I can't find the way.

In faith the driver and the horses
plod on in the narrow passage,
the right-of-way the Demons grant us
as they swarm and swarm around us,
some walking on snow and treetop,
some leaping into the storm itself.

Home, if I make it there, will not be warm
enough, nor will any bright song erase
the funereal chant of the Demons,
whose mourning rends my heart.

Bozhe moi, ding-ding-ding,
Bozhe moi, ding-ding-ding
Bozhe moi, ding-ding-ding

1830, Translation and adaptation by Brett Rutherford

HOXIE HOUSE

The high house, unpainted timbers already
blackened, was Truth and Wisdom's armory,
walls thick enough to bar the arrow
of the hostile Indian, windows so high
and leaded panes so narrow so that no sin,
however faint, could penetrate
the dim, cool classroom. "In Adam's Fall,
We Sinned All," began the alphabet. The boys
stayed on until they could sum and call out
the hymn and credo of the Pilgrim Fathers;
the girls, few and tubercular, were such
as clung to knowledge for scant hope
of ever seeing a husband, spinsters
in waiting for the church pew, the rounds
of chaste charity, if they lived. The stooped
and spectacled teacher made silence,
obedience, and the occasional slap
of an ominous birch rod his syllabus.
One early autumn day, as darkness crept
with dankness into the unfired room,
he grew distracted from his lecturing
on the certainty of Hell by two distinct
aberrancies: the clatter and fall
of chestnuts from a spreading tree
that had grown too close for comfort
to the schoolhouse, and the pale face
of Sarah, the oldest of his female charge.
Her agitation at his lecture, agitated him.
His hands began to tremble as he realized
she had come back from a necessity
(so long outdoors and back from the privy
he feared the wolves had taken her)
with a dark smear on her hands he realized
was woman's blood. She trembled, crouched
in her seat, her voice a scant whisper
as he required *amens* and recitations.

When dusk came, and the boys hurtled
toward the broad pond, the trails among
the great trees canopied with vines,
the waiting farms and close houses,
Sarah moved slowly, raising herself with hands
protectively below her waist as though
she feared a trail might follow her, a lure
to bear and beast, a stain upon the landscape.
He blocked her passage. "Stay," he said.
"Thou hast the mark of sin upon thee."
She tried to dodge him; his hands reached out
and held her by the shoulders. Her blush
was like a bonfire. She could not speak.
He led her behind the schoolhouse. Silent
she was as he found a leaf pile and pushed
her down there. "Daughter of Eve,"
he cursed her as his mouth found her lips,
"Thou art man's perdition." She cried out;
the black boards of Hoxie House, the long
dark shadow of Truth and Wisdom's armory
muffling his groans and the tumult
of the lesson he taught her. That night,
she would close her primer forever,
and take the unbibled spinster's vow.
No one would ever ask, and no one
would ever believe, how on the day
she bled first, she bled a second time.

ON THE ISLAND OF POHNPEI

Been to the ruins, have you? Not yet? I can tell
you're one of those scholarly types. Deep.
I like a firm handshake. New Englanders
come from that Innsmouth place a lot —
limp, clammy handshakes is all you get
from one o' them. I know their ways and signs
and can pass when I have to. Just slouch
and tie a scarf around your neck. Feel sorry
when I see their kids, all handsome-like,
until they grow into that "ancestral look."
Still, there are homelier types around here.
You look more Boston to me, averse
as you seem to be to sunlight. I see the way
you pick your table, one beam of light
on that book you always carry, the rest of you
in shadow. If I painted any more,
that would make a fine study. So, Harvard,
is it? you on one of those expeditions?
No, never seen anyone from Arkham before.
Miska — Miska*tonic*, you say? Can't say I ever
heard of it, though we've had scholarly types
who wouldn't say where they're from
and what they're doing. Sometimes they unload
crate after crate from the cargo ship
then hole up back and above the ruins.
Good pickings for scavengers, too, since
more than half of those fellows disappeared. Sink holes,
you see — they have a way of opening up
when you least expect it. Beneath those ruins,
no one can guess how far down it can go.
Funny thing is, there are tunnels down there
that go deep below the ocean, yet dry
as a Baptist on a blue Sunday.
A lot of those other scholars go sun-mad
or catch some funny diseases from the village girls.

One old professor, philologist I think,
said he would never sleep again,
so he razored off his eyelids. He's off
in the madhouse in Wellington. Thank you, yes,
I do know just about everybody. Used to be
you could count the white folk on two hands.

Now with the hippies and the Lovecraft tourists,
this place is getting too crowded for me.
I've done a museum's worth of paintings
in those ruins, and did a lot of diving
in my younger days. There's more of those ruins
under the water than above, you know.
Those — what do you learned folk call them —
Encylco — Yes, "Cyclopean" — that's the word
I was searching for. Funny thing is that out there
and down below, it goes so deep you could swear
it was never above water, not for a day,
so how could these Polynesians have built it?
I sold a lot of painting to visitors — the ruins,
a little wildlife, sometimes I'd get a village girl
or some boys to pose for me, very classical.
Nowadays they come and ask for tentacles.
They want that god (I'm not going to say his
name), dragging his squid face over the landscape.
I want to spit every time I hear "R'lyeh!"
Seeing as you're not one of the hippies,
I'd be happy to take you to the ruins. Easy
it is to lose your way, and as I said,
there are places that fall away. You might
even find the skeleton of one of your own professors,
ha! Just joking! You don't need to look that way.

Fact is, I want to get off this island.
A chance at a gallery in Sydney, fancy
I'd finally get to see Hong Kong or Thailand.
It's the hippies, you see, these last two years,
since the stuff they call "trans-heroin" arrived.
Nepal is practically empty and the Afghanis
are mad as hell that some unknown white powder
has pushed all other drugs aside. Now Pohnpei

is the Haight-Ashbury of the South Pacific.
They're building hostels on the beach.
Three Lebanese, ah, shall I call them
"businessmen," and some Russians, shall I call them
"silent partners," have set up a dance club there —
see the smoke? — not twenty yards from the ruins.
Since you're a scholar, and I can trust you,
I'll let you in on the secret: the white powder
comes from here, from fabled R'lyeh, Pohnpei Island.
Take it just once, and all you want to do is sleep,
and in that sleep — my god, what they tell me!
Those so-called gentle hippies. One sat there,
right where you're sitting, and boasted to me,
"Last night, in my dream, I killed a thousand men.
The powder wore off before I could finish eating them."
At first, it came from divers, not bringing up pearls,
but caked-up minerals from an outcrop,
a crazy place where those ancient stones
had fallen into something and the white
stuff, over many centuries, extruded outward.

But now the Lebanese, on the ploy of laying
a cement foundation for their nightclub
jack-hammered their way down to the vein,
the mother lode of chalk-like powder.
The Russians watch everything, sit down below
in what they call "The Kitchen," Kalashnikovs
at the ready. There goes the neighborhood.
I have to listen to the thump-thump-a-thump
of the living dead zombie dance music
some nights till three in the morning.
There's a neon sign, oh, you'll see it,
with tacky Hawaiian lettering, that reads
LOUNGE R'LYEH — HOOKAH ALL NIGHT.

Inside, the hookah pipes emerge
from the floor below, where, in the "kitchen,"
three idiot village girls tend to the charcoal
burner, the bubbling cauldron of water.
The tubes run upward and through the floor,
right to the hookah tables. And they sit,

and they sit, and they sit. The waiters
empty their pockets. Dawn comes,
and the smokers awaken outside, piled
in a heap on top of one another. They smile.
They don't even care that they've been robbed.
Each night at dusk there are more of them,
pressing against the bamboo enclosure,
waiting for the neon sign to come on.
You look agitated, professor. I guess
you didn't realize what kind of place
you've come to for your holiday. It's fine,
I guess, to spend your days afield.
The ruins, yes, the ruins are beautiful.
You just don't want to be here at night.
Did I mention the suicides? The beach,
when the tide comes in, is not so wholesome.
Drug tourists must, of necessity, exhaust
their bank accounts, and so they hope to join
the ranks of those who never awaken.
The Russians remove the bodies by noon.
Bad for business, you see.

Sooner or later they'll just export the stuff.
They'll close the lounge. Instead, a kind
of factory will sit there, extracting and packaging.
Oh, you're a wry one. What's that you said?
"Unless what's down below awakens."
Don't tell me you're one of those Believers
in that thing whose name I won't pronounce.
All right, all right, let go of me! I'll say it:
Cthulhu, Cthulhu, Cthulhu, damn you!
They're what? No, don't make me think that,
don't make me say that. You're hurting me!
Fine! Just calm down now. I heard you.
I wish I hadn't heard you.
They're ... smoking ... the ...brains ... of ... Cthulhu.

PROVIDENCE NOCTURNE: TWO PORTRAITS

TUGBOAT MAN

He rides an old tugboat, slathered in scum,
a stubby, inelegant craft, good only
for pushing or pulling, decades unpainted,
its underside roiled with barnacles.
He owns a fleet of them, proud
amid the beer-can condom flotsam
of the shallow bay. Little of note
enters this harbor without his help.
Oil tankers, ocean liners, barges laden
with toxic ash or scrap or lumber,
all lost without his men there, tugging,
pulling, day and night, fair and foul.

He squints for his hated rival, that upstart,
for two old families ply the upper Bay,
each in its own eyes the elder, the better.
Their captains' proud tonnage slides by
and even at near collision no nod, no hoot
of the horn acknowledges the other.
Each waits to buy the other out
at the Grim Reaper's auction house.

Strange he seems in his suit and tie,
one of those New England faces
with skin pinched tight as a drumhead.
He has just come from his club,
the ancestral, restricted one
from whose leather chairs the scions
of older families chide those of the younger,
and the cowed waiters dare not confuse
the pecking order in the dining room.

*Me first. My family was here
with Roger Williams. He's just
a johnny-come-carpetbagger.
I won't touch* The New York Times
if he's pawed through it first.

The talk had been, as usual,
about those god-damn interlopers —
Jews on the library board, Italians
helping to run the historical society,
women running amuck. "Don't ask me
to kiss the ring of that Episcopal bishop,
a woman! a woman! Next thing you know,
they'll be marrying lesbians, and men to men!"

On the tugboat, everything seems clear:
the clean, colonial line of the hill,
those proper white steeples, those mansions
from the days of rum, Negroes and molasses,
when business was business and it was
nobody's business what you bought or sold.
Up at the college with its Greek-front halls
they once taught Latin and Greek and classics.
Look at it now! A woman in charge, a Negress!
Marxist professors! Tattooed coeds! Hipping
and hopping with language unfit to hear!
Out of the closet perverts running the city!
And now the damn Indians everywhere,
dancing on the Arcade steps, wanting their land back!

He looks west, where once good people lived,
streets full of fine Victorian houses.
He shouts at the hulking hills: "Niggers!
Spics and Niggers! Wogs and Slant-Eyes!"
But his voice only reaches the hurricane barrier,
his only audience the wharf rats and one
whom they call —

THE FISH MAN

Everyone has seen him. In fact, your arrival
in Providence is marked by the first encounter.
We always ask newcomers:
"Have you seen the fish man yet?"
His head is conical, and bright red,
mottled, hairless, shiny as an apple,
icthyc and chinless with horrible lips.
One of his ears is twice the size
of the other, and webbed as well.
Fish man, *the Innsmouth look*,
we think as he hurtles by
on a bicycle stripped of gears and brakes.
Stand in his way and he calls out
epithets amid a cloud of spittle.
Odd job man, he may be the one
who washes your plates in the unseen kitchen,
   the one who comes in by the back door only.
His furtive broom might clean the pier
    long after closing time,
behind the seafood restaurant,
before he glides away
    into the rat and 'possum night.

He's tried all the invisible jobs in town:
an undertaker's assistant, perhaps —
his hands might be the last to touch you
as he places your body gently
on the furnace conveyor belt.
Has he done the night watch?
    the lobster shift at some printery?
Too bad
there are no more mad scientists to serve!

Who knows where he sleeps,
   or who mothered him?
What's in his mind? Has he an erotic life,
a round of afternoon lovers,
millionaires' wives who moan for him?
Does he have a library card?
Has he secretly memorized all of Milton?
Does he have a fondness for lilacs,
fireflies, and gibbous moons?
Has he ever heard of H. P. Lovecraft?

He is descended from one
of the oldest families,
could take his place,
   if he wanted,
at the club on Benevolent Street.

But we know him only by his kid-cruel nickname,
as we recount to one another
the odd frisson of a *Peckerhead sighting*.

A YEAR AND A DAY

A year since last I saw you. No: a year and a day.
The round red sun struck an octave falling,
rung out the interval as turning earth
returned to the self-same place in its orbit:
and what should happen, but nothing at all.
Nothing, or rather, another day void
to add to a year of days without you,
the same fields dressed up in the same green trees,
the same indifferent sky accepting bursts
of egomaniacal seedpods
attempting escape velocity.

During the year, I fled the quotidian,
twisting with maple propellers,
out and upward to the highest cirrus.
I sought the place of your waiting
somewhere in orbit beneath the Dog Star.
All too soon I fell, repelled
by a single graze of your cheekbones.

I thought the sun, unbent by atmosphere,
would melt your cold heart;
the rain that came
we mistook for a sign of advent —
o roots, o tendrils, o new shoots twining,
abandoned as abruptly
to summer's drought,
to hoarfrost cold,
and now, to this barren anniversary.

Each height I sought
you had already abandoned.

Each bloom thrust up —
whether the frail violet
    or the tight-fisted peony,
beautiful to me only
in some resemblance, passing,
to some aspect of you —
fell petal by petal to cindered ash.
Earth's autumn hecatombs
were burned in vain at your altar.

I know you were always there,
just one horizon beyond me,
hurrying on, pursued, and pursuing
(I dread to name whom or what!)
Must I follow you to desert rim,
to the unforgiving edge of the glacier,
to the *Mere de Glace* where Monster
and Maker (for what else are lover
and beloved?) meet once,
soliloquize and part, sworn enemies?

For a year and a day you have fled me —
(Ah! it is a year and a day, times thirty now!) —
and still the secret lives, as flowers shriek
in fields the winds italicize with longing,
in wan birch forests that topple and fall
at your departing slant. The secret lives;
the long count of calendar days resumes,
and we (myself and all things living)
tread on in quest of that one contrary wind
that would be harbinger of your return.
I will not die waiting, but *you* will wait
'til your own death to plumb regret's full sea.
Green things will bloom, mute, melancholic, doomed,
beneath a kettle of iron-gray storm-clouds.
Life will go on somehow, though gods are fled
and I, of words and love, am but a ghost.

WHAT SHE WAS LIKE

In October, he came home to stay.
Last night, as chill November ripped
the last red remnants from the maples,
and Orion stalked the horizon
he told her, "Mother,
I have to leave. I am returning
to Florida. I can't explain."

It was all he could do to get the words out.
In a month he had not said a thing
of what he had to tell her.
He had called no one, content
to be driven to malls and dinners,
polite teas with her old friends
who had never been permitted
to forget his existence, though he
saw them all as a blur of old shoes,
primped hair in unnatural hues,
coats too many times out and back
to cold storage. Tanned and plump
he felt like an exotic parrot
in a town full of mummies.

They made a striking pair.
She was a beauty once, her line
    of noble cheek and chin
as proud as his own; nature
kept all her hair, and artifice
kept it black as ever, while his
had long receded, speckled with white.
Still, she carried herself well,
as if afloat above her shoes,
as if afflicted still
    with fatal allure
(once his own curse, and power).
She is Lady Madeline Usher
to his Dorian Gray.

"The cab is on its way," he tells her
as they make morning motions
upstairs, downstairs.
She does not protest. One sigh,
head droop and hand-drop
says everything: out of her sight
is out of existence. His butterfly
would fade to moth memory.
Once more, he'd be reduced
to an object of conversation:
*Art School — No, never married,
poor boy — lives far away —
I've never met his friends.*

Perhaps, from there, from the safe
distance of a letter, he could tell her.

As he packs the last suitcase,
reverse motion from a month ago,
things won't fit easily.
"You have scarcely time for breakfast,"
she admonishes from the doorway.
"I'd rather shower," he says.
"You have so many things now,"
    she says, alluding
    to all her recent gifts,
"impossible to pack them all.
This is so sudden."

Most of the clothes are in the closet.
They are dead weight, ballast
to keep his ship from sailing.
Just one new suit, an exquisite black,
he folds beneath old jeans,
khaki trousers and well-worn shirts.
It would have its use.

She mumbles something, it sounds
like "Oh, very well." She's gone.
He takes a towel and razor and soap
for his hurried shower — and then —
as though in dream's slow motion
he passes her bedroom where

two disembodied arms stretch out,
    two alabaster cylinders
    arms odalisque, surreal,
against a paisley bedspread —
no, it is a mirror laid flat on the bed,
    reflecting two arms to the elbow bared,
the door ajar, as she intended it;

he peers round to see her thrashing there,
    half-crouched, a butcher knife
before her transfixed eyes, first
    in one hand, then tightly in two,
the one-hand gesture a throat-cut sweep,
    two-handed, it turns upon herself,
    blade pointed at base of bosom,
    a disemboweling thrust if only
she would — but she doesn't.
    She looks up, sees him seeing her.
The door goes shut.

He tiptoes past, decides
    he will forego the shower.
With a great motion
    he did not think within him,
he rises, bags in both hands —
neither embrace nor handshake
a possibility as he backs
down the stairway and down
to the door; it opens somehow
behind his fumbling fingers
twisted as they are with bag-holds,
and he is out.

The full light of cloudless day,
out there, the oxygen
which seemed so lacking amid
the wallpaper and tapestries
rushes in to fill his breathing —
Is the cab on its way? —
no matter — he would turn the corner,
away and out of her sight at last.

Gone is the death-urge that brought him here
to a rust-belt town that even rust
had abandoned, as if old broth
were a cure for his tumors, as if
the thing that gnawed him
would stop gnawing if *she* forgave him
the sin of their decades' severance.

The fresh air wants to fill him.
He breathes hard breaths, short,
    then longer. No, it is still there,
odds not good if they cut him open.
He will go back to the sand and the coral,
    the indifferent tide,
the long, slow sunsets.

He pauses once, before the turn
to the safe side street, feels eyes
like spider tendrils on neck-nape.
She is there;
she has ascended to the attic,
watching,
      mouth mouthing incantations
of arachnid web-pull.

He will not turn; he will not look.
Thank God, he thinks, the mad
do not go forth. They stay at home,
tethered to memory and failure,
eyes fixed at last on blankness,
a pale face in a rhomboid window.

THAT MOMENT

A prisoner in Stalin's camps kept this notebook, made of wood and birch bark, hidden under his straw bedding. He wrote on this page, from memory, a 1917 poem by Anna Akhmatova. Below, I have made my own version of the poem followed by a few lines of my own about the photo.

I know precisely when it happened —
Monday, the twenty-first. At night,
the roofs of the city enshrouded in mist —
and what — some idling fool decided
there was a thing in the world called love.

And look at us — from boredom
or laziness, we bought the lie
and we live it thus: daily we
look forward to meetings; nightly
we dread the moment of parting.
And, oh, we fall slaves
to every passing love song.

But, gradually, this thing I know
will be passed on to everyone,
and a hush will descend.
I figured this out by accident,
and since, have parted ways
from the self I was formerly.
                    —Anna Akhmatova, 1917

★★★★

Somewhere, a nameless man,
a cipher in an unmapped gulag,
makes, and conceals
   beneath his dank straw bed,
a birch-bark notebook.
With god knows only what for ink
he writes this poem from memory.
"Akhmatova," he sighs. "I love her."
They have never met. Her bleak work
and its desolating music
his one last link to things of beauty.

LINES OVERHEARD

Behind a freshman couple
on the first day of classes:
*Well, if anybody bothers us,
there can always be an accident.*

On Thayer Street, behind a girl
who has drawn with ball-point pen
fake track marks on both her arms:
Once, I drank rubbing alcohol.

Heard on my doorstep
through the closed door:
*I'm just going to rob and rob
until somebody stops me.*

At Eddie's Diner, amid a lull
in table talk, one voice
of four Italian businessmen:
*So who's gonna do this —
your hit man or mine?*

INTRO TO LITERARY THEORY

1
The poem is
the poem
is what it is
precisely

self-explicating,
its DNA code
repeating itself
endlessly.

The poem is the poem,
a dull virus,
a one-door
mousetrap

2
For you, my friend,
the poem is
the poem,

is everything
we know in common,
the books and symphonies
we hold between us.

When I write
"bell," or "tree,"
you know which one —
"beloved" and "gone,"
the same fierce arrow
transfixes both
    of us.

3
The poem is
the poem
in secret.

The seed of crystal
is *not* the crystal.

What all this means
is none of your
damn
business.

OLD POET GLIMPSED
ON THE SUBWAY

At 5 p.m. on a Monday night
on a subway car at Wall Street,
amid the pack and crush of crowds
I glimpse once more the old poet.

One arm bent round upon itself —
a stroke had crippled him.
His suit and tie, though loose and rumpled
says everything: serf now
to a fiefdom of profit-taking.
The great light of his eyes
    had gone out.
There was no more panther in him,
and the shrill gulls
    had taken his words.

He was always more prey than poet.
Hard boys would follow him
home from the bank each payday,
spying his shambling gait
from stoop front and alleyway,
tapping their fists
against their open palms
anticipating an easy gain.

His bosses marked him
as a man they need not advance,
a reliable cipher
likely to die at his desk.
They never knew
his tapping fingers
were not assisting
his eyes' summing
of a column of numbers,
but counting syllables
of a quietly-mumbled sonnet,

or that he once spent his nights
in lofts and cafes and poetry salons
where his tremulous voice,
drunk on Dylan Thomas,
contended for laurels.

Now on the hurtling train,
as the stops are called
and derelicts shuffle-sway
amid the well-dressed brokers,
he does not look up from his reading
(if the price of mutual funds
      can be called reading).
Perhaps he dreads the gaze
of the predatory mugger,
or worse, the inquisitive eye
of a poet who remembers him.

I leave the car. It hurtles on.
I doubt our paths will cross again..

Years back I had published his first,
    and only,
        book.

YOUNG GIRL'S PRAYER TO EOS, AT CORINTH

I pray to rosy-fingered dawn,
the goddess Eos,
for a good day. Today
especially, I need the luck.

Nothing about our family
is like any other family.
It starts with *her*. I call her mama.
She calls me *daughter*,
and other endearments:
*my little ransom, my lock
of golden ram-fleece,
my little vindication.*
My real name a murmur only
as she prays for herself and for me,
to the floor-crack goddess
whose name is contagion
to even utter aloud.

The old nurse Iole calls her "mistress,"
and fears her tantrums,
her whip-snaps over rusty water
or herbs picked in haste
without their medicinal roots.
Yet mama takes counsel
from the only countrywoman she has
among these Attic strangers.
What would she do if Iole
were not there to hold her back?
I dread to think it.

Only papa calls her by name —
always a trembling vocative
as though she were a goddess,
each glance or word or embrace
a begged-for beneficence.

As it should be,
considering our lineage,
daughters of kings.

Just days ago he called to me.
I ran to meet him. *Beware
your mother*, he warned me.
*When her eyes go all black
the way they do most every day now,
I want you to run and hide.*

Of course I didn't.
I do the eye thing, too,
but not as well as my mother does.

Just yesterday, beneath the oak,
on the hilltop in view of the palace
mama and I made a little hecatomb,
and as she watched and said the words,
I burned the effigy of the king,
and a blond-haired doll
to represent his daughter.

And papa? I asked,
thrusting the helmeted doll
head first into the twig-fire,
shall we burn papa?

She seized the doll and squeezed it.
No, she said. *Not papa.*
And she held it to her bosom,
eyes closed and rocking,
so long that I crept away.
Let me never love anyone
if it hurts that much!

Another day, fair Eos
of the day's dawning.
I bend to kiss your saffron robe.
Promise me the sight of sunrise
tomorrow, and all will be well.

For this is the day
of my initiation: the world below,
and the one above both joined
in a terrible drama.

And thus it shall play out:

She is calling us.
Children, children, come!
I tremble and look at my brother.
She is at the doorway,
her eyes all black, her arms
extended rigidly.
Darker, lower, her voice again:
Children, children come! Now!
I push my brother,
the golden-locked fool. *You first*,
I say. He runs to her embrace.
I watch what she does.
It is over quickly, as with a chicken
or a hare. *Come daughter,
come!* she beckons me.

I step over my brother. It is my turn.
My eyes go to Hecate. I lift
my throat and take in my grasp
my mama's trembling knife-hand.

I know I am there. I know
a crimson ribbon is leaving me
and flooding everywhere.
I hear the howl of a man.
It is papa. He has seen it.
I hear the long, low laughter
as mama mocks him.

Then, in a while I shall do
what mama taught me well.
My eyes will return from Hecate,
and the ribbon of my blood
will furl back inward,
and I shall be whole again.

Who bides for this day,
O fair and early-rising Eos,
and begs for another dawn tomorrow?
I am Medea, daughter of Medea.
And my daughter who comes after
will be Medea, daughter of Medea.
And we will make men sorry
they were ever born.

FOUR POEMS OF LI YÜ

DOWN SOUTH

After the Chinese of Li Yü (d. 978 CE)

Down South, they know what to do with springtime.
There, when my thoughts turn away
    from duty and empire, I imagine myself,
where the spring is already in progress.
Pleasure boats are in every lake now,
    the *er-hu* fiddles a-hum, the flute girls
exchanging shy looks with the young scholars.
The green-faced rivers are drunk with willows,
towns dust-clogged with their yellow catkins,
more flowers abloom than eye or hand can capture.
Busy are those who adore this blossoming,
    busier still their sleepless nights of loving.

FISHERMAN

After the Chinese of Li Yü (d. 978 CE)

1
My bark is but a leaf,
no oar
but the will
of the errant spring breeze,
this way, that way.
A loose line of fishing string,
on its end a light hook
might serve as rope
and anchor.
The destination:
that flower-covered islet.
The prize:
 an icy cask of wine.

Since nothing here is what it is,
but what it stands for,
one or ten thousand waves,
one or ten thousand realms,
what do they matter?

I do not need the island.
I do not, at the moment, crave
the plum green savor of wine.
I have my freedom.

2
Water, the chemist says,
is incompressible.
The delicate waves,
invisible and relentless,
a unity, break up
a thousand-piled layer
of warlike snowflakes.
They never stood a chance.
Now comes the onslaught:
cloud upon cloud upon cloud
of plum and peach and cherry
bannermen from Spring's
inevitable and drumless army
throw themselves down
upon the snowbanks.
White mists enshroud
the waiting wine cask.
I sit with fishing rod and line.
One season has fought and won,
one season has held, and died.
I am doing nothing. Who else
could be as happy as I am?

EXILE, UNDER THE NEW MOON

Adapted from the Chinese of Li Yü

I know I should go in, now.
It is best to forget it all, better to sleep
and recall it to ghost-life; least-best
is waiting out the night here,
thinking of those who have gone.
The wind is back in the courtyard
(new wind or ever the same one?)
and the dull grass is sliced
    with new green slivers.
Spring, undeniable, paints yellow-green
    in willow shoots.
Long I recline on the balustrade,
waving away my servant, a nay
to the tonic of the waiting teacup.

I am alone. I am not
reciting old poems. My mouth
is clamped with the forgetting
of mere words. All ears,
I wait for for the next west-east
fluttering amid the bamboo leaves,
wind of a new moon as always.
Away, where I am missed
and amid those I despair of,
exactly the same sky shivers.

Rubbing their hands
    together, the pi-pa players
await my orders. What tune
can I order amid the willow rush,
the ruffle of wind in the cat-tails?
I gesture them to stillness. They bow.

Old Chen, I see, has not removed
the hundred-year-old wine jar,
nor my ink pot and its brushes.
As for calligraphy, what is mine
against that cracked-ice poem
that just now melts on the lake face.

On the deep, dark terrace behind me
burns a single candle, one ember
beside it, last incense breath.
The past. The past. The dawn
that I am facing is solitary;
there seems scant need to undress
but to rise and re-dress again,
for whom, or for what?
I feel in my hair the gnawing frost,
as on my brow the last snow
hovers at edge of vision
and refuses to melt.
I   will   just   sit.
Thought is unthinkable.

ASSIGNATION

    after a Chinese poem by Li Yü

The flowers were bright
   (and might have lit my way like lanterns)
but the moon was diffused in light mist.
Cool, but not too cold,
that was the best night to go to my lover.
Trembling I trod the perfumed stones,
step upon step amid the night-blooms.
I held in one hand the golden-threaded shoes,
in the other his scroll of urgent summoning.

South of the newly-painted hall,
in the appointed place I met him.
His face was turned away and upward
as though he searched the moon face
or with his hawk-fierce eye some dove
asleep on a still and leafy branchlet.
At first, I leaned against him, shivering;
my pale arms could not encompass
the sweep of his cloaked broad shoulders.
He made a sound that might have been
my name, or a sighing exhalation.
I said, "I cannot come as often now,
so tonight you must love me twice as hard."

ABOUT THE POEMS

THE SPECIAL WARD AT BUTLER HOSPITAL was premiered at Lovecraft's grave, with a number of attendees from the 2013 Necronomicon conference present. A few may have squirmed to realize that I was mocking those demented fans who actually think they *are* H.P. Lovecraft. There are more of them every year, walking around in old suits, disdaining everything modern, and living on canned chili, beans and crackers. This is pretty much my farewell to HPL fandom.

TRILOBITES were the dominant life form on earth for hundreds of millions of years. This poem speculates that they may have been around long enough to develop a kind of gestalt consciousness, customs and history, despite the fact that they could most likely only produce clicking noises and bubbling sounds in lieu of speech. I have been fascinated with trilobites since childhood, and especially since finding myself on a train next to a paleontologist who was carrying fossil specimens of triloblites with their legs and feelers intact. When I premiered the poem, I used castanets for the clicking sounds.

AT INNSMOUTH HARBOR is an impressionistic piece inspired, of course, by the imaginary seacoast town in Lovecraft's tale, "The Shadow Over Innsmouth."

THE DEMONS is my adaptation of Pushkin's famous poem. I have added the driver's exclamations of "Bozhe moi" (My God!), as well as the sound of the ringing sleigh bell.

Visiting HOXIE HOUSE in Sandwich with my friends David and Kleber, as part of a fast tour of pre-1700 houses in New England, I found the color, geometry, and tiny windows of the house, which had been a schoolhouse at one point, oppressive and disquieting. In an instant, the events depicted in this poem came to me almost as a vision.

ON THE ISLAND ON POHNPEI takes place on the South Pacific island whose Cyclopean ruins inspired both Abraham Merritt and H.P. Lovecraft. Certainly the island depicted in "The Call of Cthulhu" was inspired by contemporaneous accounts of Pohnpei. I also used the poem to convey my disdain and disgust for hookah bars.

PROVIDENCE NOCTURNE: TWO PORTRAITS may be a composite of various characters encountered in Providence. Very little of it is imagined. Any resemblance to persons living or dead is of course coincidental.

A YEAR AND A DAY is a revision of a poem about obsessive love. Many will recognize themselves in its lines. Some emotions cannot be escaped.

WHAT SHE WAS LIKE was in my last collection, but I continue to tinker with it. It came to me as a complete experience, in a dream, one of those dreams in which I was inside someone else's body.

THAT MOMENT is explained by its own epigraph. The photograph of the Akhmatova poem written on birch bark by a prisoner, has haunted me for years.

LINES OVERHEARD tells in brief what the common folk in Providence are like. We have the highest rate of untreated mental illness in America, and the highest rate of drug addiction. And as for crime, the state's motto has long been said to be "Mobsters and Lobsters."

I do not know when I wrote INTRO TO LITERARY THEORY. I took my first undergraduate course in critical theory in 2003, so I may have written it then. It just came to light.

OLD POET GLIMPSED ON THE SUBWAY is a further revision of a piece in my last collection. Tinkering with tenses makes it clearer.

Anticipating the English National Theatre broadcast of Euripides' *Medea*, a new poem came to me almost line-for-line as I walked down College Hill to work. In a flash I had altered the myth so that Medea had a son and a daughter, instead of two sons. YOUNG GIRL'S PRAYER TO EOS, AT CORINTH is the result. The title and opening stanzas will suggest the context to those familiar with the drama; for others, the horror of the story unveils more gradually. An elitist, I assume at least that my readers who know Medea was.

FOUR POEMS OF LI YÜ. Li Yü was the last emperor of Southern Tang. He lost his kingdom and went into exile. The first Sung emperor, a poet himself, was so jealous of Li Yü's poems that he sent a messenger with poisoned wine, which he was ordered to drink on the spot. The intensity of loss and longing in the exile's writings rise to an intensity not commonly found in Chinese poetry. These are my loose adaptations. In the last poem, "Assignation," the poet assumes the voice of a young girl or concubine.

— BRETT RUTHERFORD
Providence, Rhode Island
October 16, 2014

ABOUT THE POET

Brett Rutherford, born in Scottdale, Pennsylvania, began writing poetry seriously during a stay in San Francisco. During his college years at Edinboro State College in Pennsylvania, he published an underground newspaper and printed his first hand-made poetry chapbook. He moved to New York City, where he founded The Poet's Press in 1971. For more than twenty years, he worked as an editor, journalist, printer, and consultant to publishers and nonprofit organizations.

After a literary pilgrimage to Providence, Rhode Island, on the track of H.P. Lovecraft and Edgar Allan Poe, he moved there with his press. *Poems From Providence* was the fruit of his first three years in the city (1985-1988), published in 1991. Since then, he has written a study of Edgar Allan Poe and Providence poet Sarah Helen Whitman (briefly Poe's fiancee), a biographical play about Lovecraft, and his second novel, *The Lost Children* (Zebra Books, 1988). His poetry, in volumes both thematic and chronological, can be found in *Poems From Providence* (1991, 2011), *Things Seen in Graveyards* (2007), *Twilight of the Dictators* (1992, 2009), *The Gods As They Are, On their Planets* (2005, 2012), *Whippoorwill Road: The Supernatural Poems* (1998, 2005, 2012), and *An Expectation of Presences* (2012).

Returning to school for a master's degree in English, Rutherford completed this project in 2007, and worked for University of Rhode Island in distance learning, and taught for the Gender and Women's Studies Department. There, he created courses on "The Diva," "Women in Science Fiction," and "Radical American Women."

He has prepared annotated editions of Matthew Gregory Lewis's *Tales of Wonder,* the poetry of Charles Hamilton Sorley, A.T. Fitzroy's antiwar novel *Despised and Rejected,* and the four-volume collected writings of Emilie Glen.

His interests include classical music and opera, and Latin American music; Chinese art, history and literature; bicycling, graveyards, woods, horror films, intellectual history, and crimes against nature.

Retiring from his workaday life in early 2016, Rutherford moved to the Squirrel Hill neighborhood in Pittsburgh where he continues to write, study music, and run The Poet's Press.

ABOUT THIS BOOK

The body text for this book is Plantin Schoolbook. Several attractive modern fonts, including Galliard and Plantin, are based on typefaces originally designed by Robert Granjon (1513-1589), a prolific type designer and founder active in Paris, in the shop of Christoph Plantin, and later in Rome at the Vatican. In 1913, Monotype issued several versions of Plantin, based on some of Granjon's designs, including the highly legible Plantin Schoolbook, designed by Frank Hinman Pierpont. Section and main titles are set in Solemnis, a calligraphic font designed in 1953 by Günter Gerhard Lange for the Berthold Foundry. Poem titles are set in Schneidler Black. The book is also decorated with several 18th-century Dutch borders and ornaments. The Trilobite illustrations are from the work of Joachim Barrande (*Systême Silurien du Centre de la Bohême*, Paris 1872).

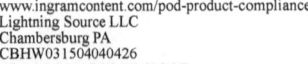
www.ingramcontent.com/pod-product-compliance
Lightning Source LLC
Chambersburg PA
CBHW031504040426
42444CB00007B/1207